Bracelet with Beaded Beads

SIZE: 7"

MATERIALS:
- 2 Capri 4mm bicone crystals
- 4 Light Topaz AB 4mm bicone crystals
- 2 Sterling Silver 3mm round beads
- 0 Sterling Silver 5mm daisy spacer beads
- Sterling Silver toggle clasp
- Sterling Silver crimp tubes
- Softflex .014 diameter beading wire
- Smoke Fireline 4 lb. test
- Size 12 Sharps beading needles

INSTRUCTIONS:

Beaded Beads:

Make 3 Blue beaded beads.

Make 2 Gold beaded beads.

Bracelet:

Refer to the photo to string the components onto beading wire.

Attach clasp and secure with crimp tubes.

Index of Projects

Tennis Bracelet

pages 8 - 9

Quilt Bracelet

pages 10 - 11

Solid Square Earrings

pages 12- 13

Zig-Zag Bracelet

pages 14 - 16

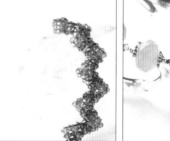

Bracelet with Square Frame

pages 16 - 17

Necklace with Rectangle

pages 18 - 19

Necklace with Circle

pages 20 - 21

Bracelet with Toggle Clasp

pages 22 - 23

Necklace with Cross

pages 24 - 27

Necklace with Triangle Bail

pages 28 - 31

Basic Supplies

Crystals and Seed Beads:

All the projects in this book are made with 3, 4 or 6 mm *Swarovski* bicone crystal beads. Because of their shape, bicone beads fit perfectly together in Right Angle Weave (RAW).

For some projects only one size of crystal works well, but for others you can make the project using different sizes. The crystal sizes are listed in each project's materials list. On any project where different sizes can be used, I have made an example so you can see what that size will look like. On those projects that can be made in more than one size, the graph is made for the colors of the larger size crystal example. Usually, it is easier to first learn a project when using larger size crystals. In the project's graphs I show the colors I used for each project, but you can play with the colors and create your own unique combinations.

You will need size 15/0 seed beads for adding loops on some of the projects. In all of the projects you have the option of adding size 15/0 seed beads between the crystals for extra embellishment. They add stability and make the piece stiffer by filling in the gaps between crystals.

Thread:

I used *Berkeley* Fireline 4 lb. test for all the projects. Crystals have sharp edges that cut thread and Fireline holds up best against their abrasiveness. Fireline also makes the beadwork stiffer, which is very important for most of these projects.

If you choose not to make multiple thread passes through the crystals, you should use Fireline 6 lb. test instead. It will help give stiffness to the pieces. Fireline comes in Smoke and Crystal colors. In each project I tell which Fireline color complements those bead colors. Unless the bead colors are light, Smoke usually looks the best.

Needles:

I prefer size 12 sharps English beading needles because they don't break and bend like the longer needles. If you feel more comfortable with the longer size 12 needles, use them instead. I find size 15 English beading needles helpful when making multiple passes through the crystals and to add 15/0 seed beads between the crystals. If the needle won't pass through a bead, switch to a smaller needle or go through a different bead. Note: Because crystals can break, be careful not to force the needle through the bead.

Scissors:

You need high quality embroidery scissors with a fine, sharp point.

Glue:

If you choose to glue your knots, I find that the best glue is G-S Hypo cement. It has a very tiny applicator, but you can also use a beading needle to apply the glue to the knot. I did not use glue on any of the projects in this book, because I didn't like how it looked if glue got on the crystals.

Crimping and Stringing:

To make the components into finished jewelry I strung them on flexible beading wire (Soft Flex .014 diameter - 21 strands) and used crimp tubes and crimping tool.

Additional Materials

Scotch tape • Lap desk or work surface with a piece of Vellux to keep the beads from rolling away • Needle-nose pliers to help pull the needle through the beads • Small triangle trays or porcelain bead dishes to separate and sort the beads • Wire cutter • Ruler or measuring tape • Assorted beads, clasps, ear wires and wire for making the components into finished jewelry.

Basic Instructions

Starting and Finishing Threads:

Cut thread 1 - 2 yards when starting a project, because the less thread you have to add, the better.

If you are not comfortable using thread that long, use a shorter length.

Approximately 8" from one thread end, place a small piece of Scotch tape around the thread to keep the beads from falling off when you start weaving.

Remove the tape when the first beads have been secured.

Thread a needle on the other end.

Adding Thread:

When your working thread is down to 3 - 4 inches, you will need to stop and add a new thread.

Cut and tape a new length of thread and weave it through a few beads in the piece, exiting out of the same bead that the last working thread is coming out of.

Continue beading.

Tie off the thread ends as you go, or wait until you finish weaving the whole piece.

Note: If you have thread leftover when you finish weaving the project side, use it to weave the edge instead of starting a new thread.

Finishing a Thread:

Take the needle through a crystal and under the threads between the crystal you are exiting and the next crystal.

Then take the needle through the loop of thread this has formed, going over the thread that you had sewed under before. Pull tight.

Then pass through the next crystal and make another knot.

I recommend making at least 2 - 3 knots.

After the last knot, pass through the next crystal and cut off the excess thread as close to the crystal as possible.

Multiple Thread Passes:

In the weaving instructions and diagrams I show passing through the crystals one time. You should actually go through every crystal multiple times to reinforce and stiffen the beadwork. I recommend at least 3 – 4 passes.

The only projects in this book that require flexibility are the Crystal Tennis Bracelet, Quilt Bracelet and Zig Zag bracelet.

To avoid breaking crystals on the multiple passes, switch to a size 15 beading needle when the bead holes feel too tight for the size 12 needle, especially when using 3 mm crystals.

Remember, you also have to leave room in the crystal holes to add the edge crystals and seed bead loops and embellishments. You can pass back through the crystals as you add them or wait until the whole piece is finished. Note: It is easier to reinforce the sides before you join them together with the edge. If you choose not to make multiple passes, use Fireline 6 lb. instead of Fireline 4 lb. Keep the tension tight throughout all the beadwork.

Basic Single Needle Right Angle Weave (RAW)

NOTE: In this book a 4-bead square is referred to as a unit.

This is the basic stitch. Adapt it to fit the pattern of the project you are working on.
You will use these instructions for the following projects:
Beaded Bead, Crystal Tennis Bracelet, Quilt Bracelet, Solid Square and Toggle Clasp Bar.

1. String crystals 1, 2, 3 and 4. Push them down to the tape. Go through crystals 1 and 2. This completes 1 unit.

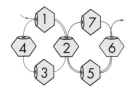

2. String crystals 5, 6 and 7. Go through crystals 2, 5 and 6.

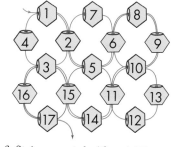

3. String crystals 8, 9 and 10. Go through crystals 6, 8, 9 and 10, turning the corner to start the second row.

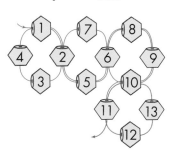

4. String crystals 11, 12 and 13. Go through crystals 10 and 11. Note: From this point you will add 3 crystals for the first unit of

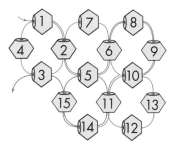

each row and 2 crystals for each following unit in that row.
5. String crystals 14 and 15. Go through crystals 5, 11, 14, 15 and 3.

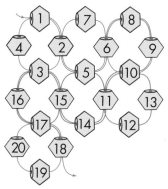

7. String crystals 18, 19 and 20. Go through crystals 17 and 18.

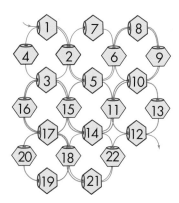

8. String crystals 21 and 22. Go through crystals 14, 18, 21, 22 and 12.

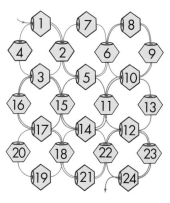

9. String crystals 23 and 24. Go through crystals 22, 12, 23 and 24.

6. String crystals 16 and 17. Go through crystals 15, 3, 16 and 17.

Basic Right Angle Weave (RAW) for Open Center Frames

This is the basic stitch. Adapt it to fit the pattern of the project you are working on.
You will use these instructions for the following projects:
Square Frame, Rectangle Frame and Toggle Clasp Square Frame.

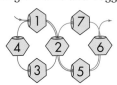

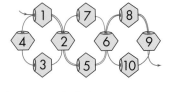

1. String crystals 1, 2, 3 and 4.
Push them down to the tape.
Go through crystals 1 and 2.

2. String crystals 5, 6 and 7.
Go through crystals 2, 5 and 6.

3. String beads 8, 9 and 10.
Go through crystals 6, 8 and 9.

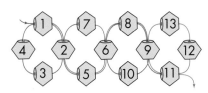

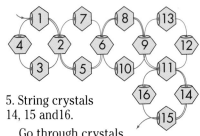

4. String crystals 11, 12 and 13.
Go through crystals 9 and 11.

5. String crystals
14, 15 and16.

Go through crystals
11, 14 and 15.

6. String crystals
17, 18 and 19.
Go through crystals
15, 17 and 18.

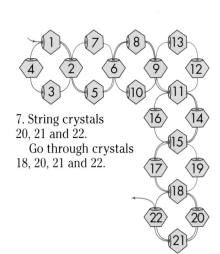

7. String crystals
20, 21 and 22.
Go through crystals
18, 20, 21 and 22.

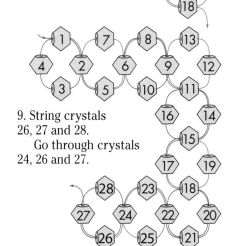

8. String crystals
23, 24 and 25.
Go through crystals
22, 23 and 24.

9. String crystals
26, 27 and 28.
Go through crystals
24, 26 and 27.

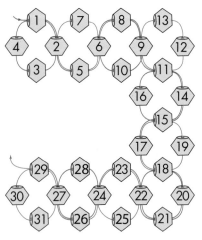

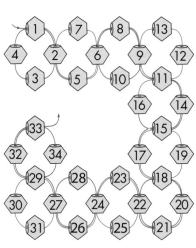

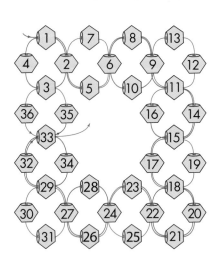

10. String crystals 29, 30 and 31.
Go through crystals 27 and 29.

11. String crystals 32, 33 and 34.
Go through crystals 29, 32 and 33.

12. String crystal 35.
Go through crystal 3. String
crystal 36. Go through crystal 33.

Basic Instructions

Finishing Components for Stringing:

The component projects in this book can be strung many different ways.

In the directions for three of the projects – the Toggle Clasp, Cross and Triangle Bail – I have included the loop instructions for hanging or stringing the piece. For all the project components, you can add a seed bead loop, leave out the corner edge crystals to create an opening or thread the wire through gaps between the crystals.

Each component project page has a finished example of one way to string the project.

If you leave out crystals to make openings for stringing – as in the finished examples for the Square and Rectangle Frames – plan ahead, because you have to leave out the crystals as you are making the edge to join together the two sides.

If you choose to add a loop, it can be attached after you finish weaving the project.

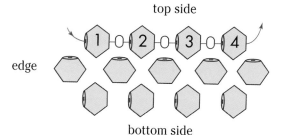

Embellishing with Seed Beads:

You have the option of adding size 15/0 seed beads in the gaps between crystals for any project in this book.

They add extra embellishment and help to stiffen the piece.

The seed beads can be added throughout the entire piece or just on one row.

For example, if you want to add seed beads to the outside row of crystals, you would take the thread through crystal 1 (see diagram), add a 15/0 seed, go through crystal 2, add a 15/0 seed, and continue until you have added seeds between all of the crystals in that row.

When you finish stringing all the seed beads, it is best to go back through them a second time.

Attaching the Edge on the 3-D Projects:

Some of the projects in this book are 3-dimensional. To accomplish this 3-D effect, you have to make two sides (front and back) and join them together with an edge.

The Solid Square, Zig Zag Bracelet, Toggle Clasp Bar and Cross have only an outside edge. The Square Frame, Rectangle Frame, Circle and Toggle Clasp Square Frame have two edges – an inside edge and an outside edge – because they have open centers.

Note: When attaching the edge on projects with open centers, it is easier to bead the inside edge first.

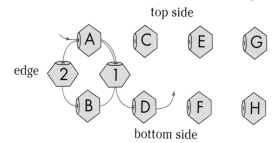

1. Stack one side on top of the other.

With the thread exiting one of the outside crystals of one of the project's sides (crystal A in the diagram), string edge crystal 1 and go through crystal B.

String edge crystal 2 and go through crystals A, 1 and D.

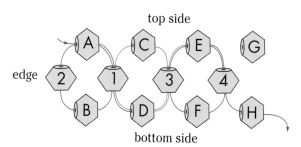

2. String edge crystal 3. Go through crystals C, 1, D, 3, and E.

String edge crystal 4 and go through crystals F, 3, E, 4 and H.

Continue in this way until the entire edge is beaded.

SIZE: 7"

MATERIALS:

- 97 Tanzanite 4mm bicone crystals
- 16 Pacific Opal 4mm bicone crystals
- 16 Lime Satin 4mm bicone crystals
- 1 gram size 15/0 matte metallic Olive Gold seed beads
- 1 gram size 15/0 matte opaque Sea Foam luster seed beads
- Smoke Fireline 4 lb. test
- Sterling Silver lobster claw clasp with soldered jump ring
- Beading needles (size 12 Sharps, size 15)

INSTRUCTIONS:

Weaving:

Using the basic Right Angle Weave instructions on page 5, weave a single row base of Tanzanite crystals 32 units long.

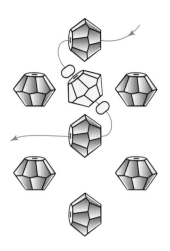

Embellishing the Top of the Base:

With the thread exiting the last crystal of the base row (center end crystal), string one Olive Gold 15/0 seed bead, one Lime Satin crystal and one Olive Gold 15/0 seed bead.

Lay the beads diagonally across the center of the unit and take the needle through the opposite side of the next center crystal on the base row.

String one 15/0 Olive Gold seed bead, one Lime Stain crystal and one 15/0 Olive Gold seed bead; go through the opposite side of the next center crystal on the base row.

Continue adding crystals and 15/0 seed beads – alternating colors - until you have added embellishment to all the units of the base row.

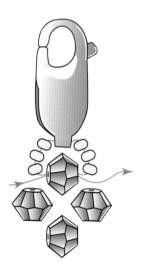

Attaching the Clasp:

With the thread exiting the last crystal on the base row (the center end bead), string three 15/0 Sea Foam seed beads, a lobster claw clasp and three 15/0 Sea Foam seed beads.

Go through the other side of the last crystal.

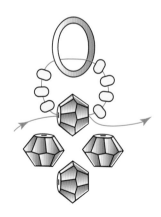

On the Other End of the Bracelet:

With the thread exiting the last crystal, string seven 15/0 Sea Foam seed bead and a soldered jump ring.

Take the needle through the other side of the last crystal.

Crystal Tennis Bracelet

Tennis bracelets got their name when Chris Evert wore a thin, in-line diamond bracelet which broke during the US Open tennis championship. The match was delayed so she could retrieve her diamonds. The name of the bracelet caught on and continues to be used today to refer to this attractive style.

The tennis bracelet derives its beauty from the glittering sparkle of this simple symmetric pattern. Right angle weave makes it easy to create a uniquely beautiful bracelet that you will be proud to wear.

Start here

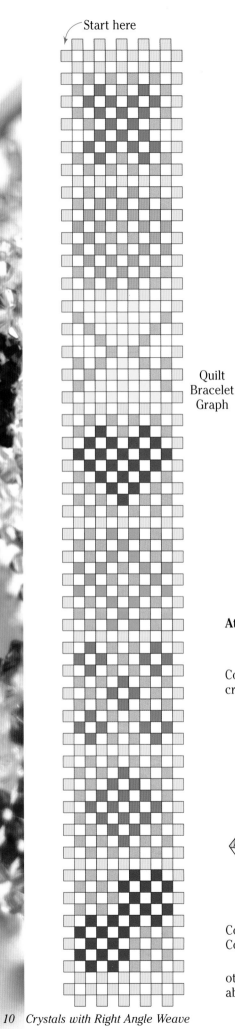

Quilt
Bracelet
Graph

Lt. Colorado Topaz

Crystal

Emerald

Rose

Topaz

Siam

Olivine

Sapphire

Amethyst

Fuchsia

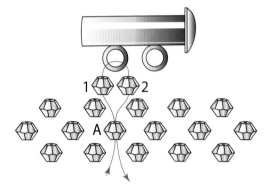

Attaching the Clasp:

Figures 1 and 2 show the last row of one end of the bracelet.

1. With the thread exiting crystal A, string crystal 1 (Lt. Colorado Topaz), go through one loop of one half of the clasp, string crystal 2 (Lt. Colorado Topaz) and go down through crystal A.

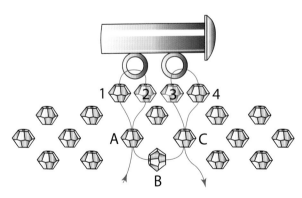

2. Take the needle through crystals B and C. String crystal 3 (Lt. Colorado Topaz), the second loop of the clasp half and crystal 4 (Lt. Colorado Topaz). Go through crystal C.

Repeat these steps for the other end of the bracelet. Attach the other half of the clasp facing the opposite direction so that it will be able to close.

SIZE: 6½"

MATERIALS:
- 155 Lt. Colorado Topaz 3mm bicone crystals
- 151 Crystal 3mm bicone crystals
- 28 Rose 3mm bicone crystals
- 24 Fuchsia 3mm bicone crystals
- 21 Siam 3mm bicone crystals
- 20 Topaz 3mm bicone crystals
- 20 Olivine 3mm bicone crystals
- 20 Sapphire 3mm bicone crystals
- 20 Emerald 3mm bicone crystals
- 16 Amethyst 3mm bicone crystals
- Crystal Fireline 4lb. test
- 2-strand Sterling Silver slide clasp
- Beading needles (size 12 Sharps, size 15)

INSTRUCTIONS:

Weaving:

Using the basic Right Angle Weave instructions on page 5 and the Quilt graph, weave a bracelet 5 units wide and 42 units long.

Quilt Bracelet

With patterns reminiscent of a Sampler Quilt, this appealing bracelet stirs up all the warm and cuddly emotions associated with the quilts that Grandma lovingly crafted.

Continue the tradition of fine craftsmanship, caring, and sharing by making the Quilt Bracelet as a gift for those you hold most dear. This alluring bracelet promises to become a treasured family heirloom.

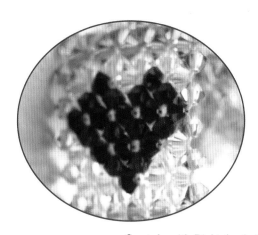

3mm bicone crystals   4mm bicone crystals

Solid Square Earrings

SIZE: 2¹/4" long

MATERIALS:

Lime Green and Teal Solid Squares:

    72 Emerald 4mm bicone crystals

    32 Peridot 4mm bicone crystals

    16 Light Topaz AB 4mm bicone crystals

    Smoke Fireline 4lb. test

    Beading needles (size 12 Sharps, size 15)

Earrings:

    2 Crystal AB 5.5x11mm Crystal drop pendants

    2 Peridot 4mm bicone crystals

    40 Matte Opaque Dark Green seed beads - 15/0

    2 Sterling Silver earwires

    6" Sterling Silver wire - 24 gauge

INSTRUCTIONS:

Solid Squares

    Make 2 Solid Squares.

Earrings:

    To add a seed bead loop, refer to the Attaching Loop instructions for the Toggle Clasp Square Frame project on page 23.

INSTRUCTIONS:

Weaving:

    Using the basic Right Angle Weave instructions on page 5 and the Solid Square Side graph, weave 2 square sides.

Attaching the Edge:

    Refer to Attaching the Edge instructions on page 7.

    Stack one side on top of the other. With the thread exiting one outside crystal on one of the sides, start in one corner to join the two sides together. Use Metallic Blue crystals for the edge.

Attaching the Loop:

    If you want to add a seed bead loop as in the finished example earrings, refer to the Attaching Loop instructions for the Toggle Clasp Square Frame project on page 23.

Solid Square

Next time you need a special focal bead, pendant, pin, or earring design, consider the elegance and simplicity of the square.

Clean lines and and dramatic color possibilities have long attracted artists to use squares to make bold, graphic pieces with a weight worthy of adorning royalty as well as delicate crystalline structures that scintillate in the captured glow of a candlelit dinner.

These pieces are so beautiful you will want to use them often, and because the color choices are endless, each project will retain its unique charm.

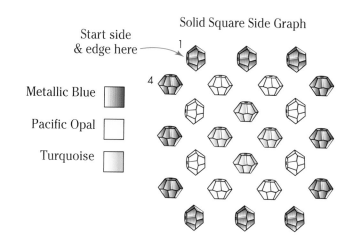

Solid Square Side Graph

Start side & edge here → 1

4

Metallic Blue

Pacific Opal

Turquoise

SIZE: 3/4" x 3/4"

MATERIALS FOR 4MM BLUE SOLID SQUARE:

Note: this square can also be made with 3mm bicone crystals.

    36 Metallic Blue 4mm bicone crystals (or Burgundy 3mm)

    16 Pacific Opal 4mm bicone crystals (or Rose Alabaster 3mm)

    8 Turquoise 4mm bicone crystals (or Crystal Copper 3mm)

    Smoke Fireline 4lb. test

    Beading needles (size 12 Sharps, size 15)

TIP: This project can be used as a diamond or a square.

With the thread exiting the last center crystal (A) at the end of one of the zig-zag sides, string nine 15/0 seed beads and one half of the clasp.

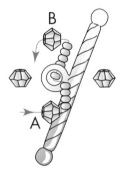

1. Take the needle through the end crystal (B) on the second zig-zag side.

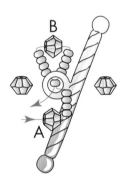

2. String four 15/0 seed beads and take the needle through the center bead of the nine 15/0 seed beads previously strung and through the loop of the clasp.

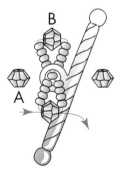

3. String four 15/0 seed beads and go through the crystal (A) on the first zig-zag side.

On the other end of the bracelet, attach the second half of the toggle clasp according to the previous instructions.

Start the sides and adding the edge here

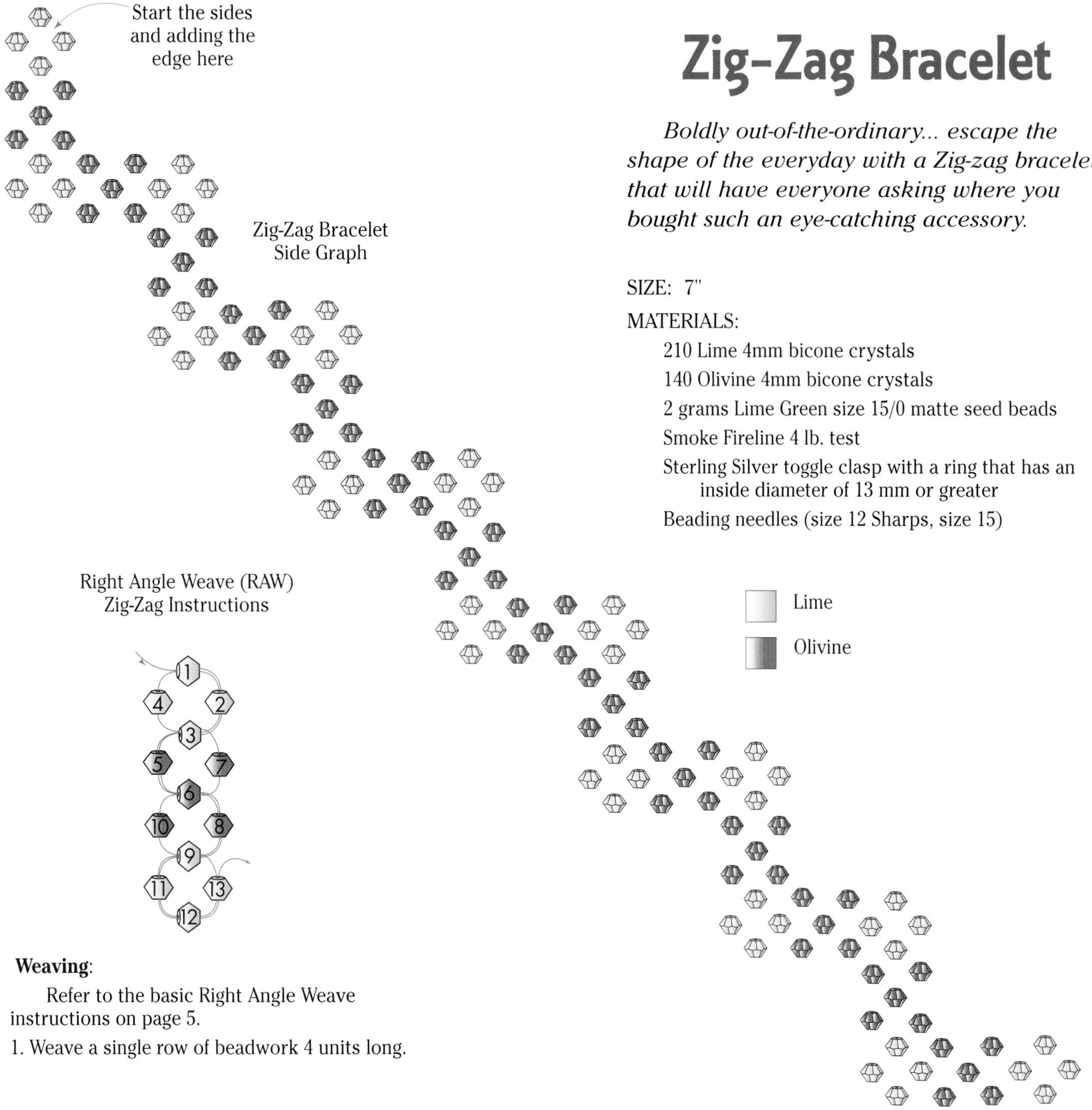

Zig-Zag Bracelet
Side Graph

Right Angle Weave (RAW)
Zig-Zag Instructions

Zig-Zag Bracelet

Boldly out-of-the-ordinary... escape the shape of the everyday with a Zig-zag bracelet that will have everyone asking where you bought such an eye-catching accessory.

SIZE: 7"

MATERIALS:

  210 Lime 4mm bicone crystals

  140 Olivine 4mm bicone crystals

  2 grams Lime Green size 15/0 matte seed beads

  Smoke Fireline 4 lb. test

  Sterling Silver toggle clasp with a ring that has an inside diameter of 13 mm or greater

  Beading needles (size 12 Sharps, size 15)

  ☐ Lime

  ▨ Olivine

Weaving:

  Refer to the basic Right Angle Weave instructions on page 5.

1. Weave a single row of beadwork 4 units long.

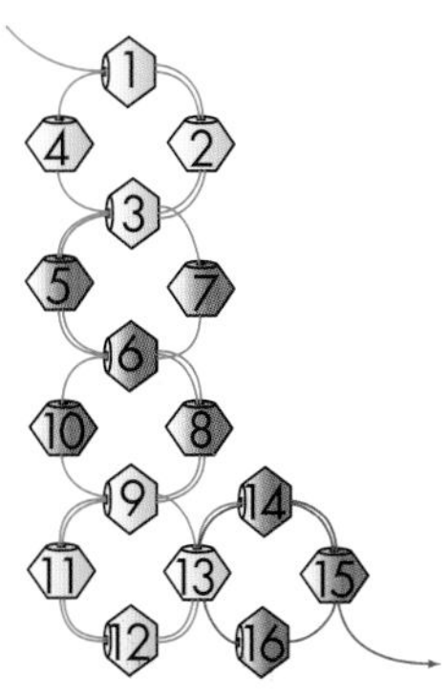

2. With the thread exiting crystal 13, string crystals 14, 15 and 16.

  Go through crystals 13, 14 and 15.

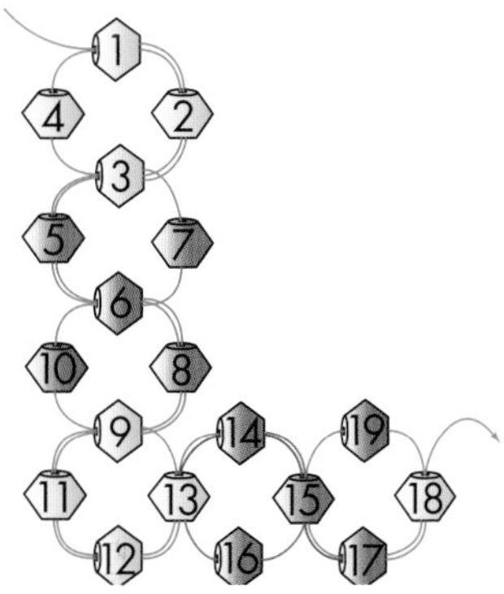

3. String crystals 17, 18 and 19.

  Go through crystals 15, 17 and 18.

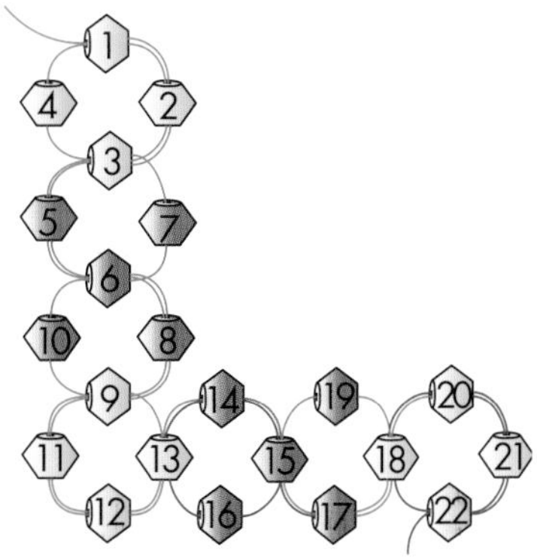

4. String crystals 20, 21 and 22.

  Go through crystals 18, 20, 21 and 22.

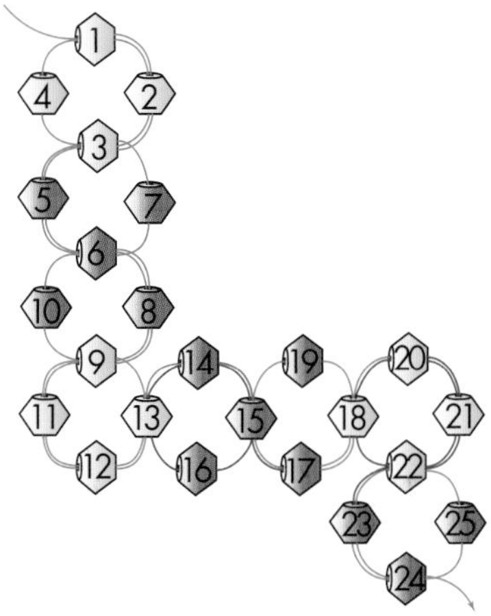

5. String crystals 23, 24 and 25.
  Go through crystals 22, 23 and 24.

Right Angle Weave (RAW)
Zig-Zag Instructions (continued)

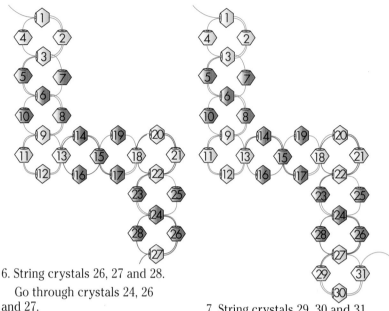

6. String crystals 26, 27 and 28.
   Go through crystals 24, 26 and 27.

7. String crystals 29, 30 and 31.
   Go through crystals 27, 29, 30 and 31.

8. String crystals 32, 33 and 34.
   Go through crystals 31, 32 and 33.

Continue with these directions following the pattern until the length of your bracelet matches the Zig-Zag side graph.

Attaching the Edge:

Refer to the Attaching the Edge instructions on page 7. Use Lime crystals for the edges. Stack one side on top of the other. With the thread exiting one crystal on one of the sides, start at one end to join the two sides together. Attach the second edge

Embellishment:

Refer to Adding Seed Bead Embellishment on page 7. Add 15/0 seed beads between crystals on both sides of the bracelet.

INSTRUCTIONS:

Weaving:

Using the basic RAW Frame instructions on page 6 and the Square Frame Side graph, weave 2 square frame sides.

Start with this end

Square Frame Outside Edge Graph

Palace Green Opal

Mint Alabaster

Ruby

Start the sides and the outside edge here.

Start the inside edge here.

Square Frame Side Graph

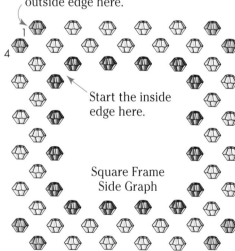

Attaching the Edge:

Refer to Attaching the Edge instructions on page 7. Use Ruby crystals for the inside edge. Stack one side on top of the other. With the thread exiting one crystal on one of the sides, start in one corner on the inside of the square to join the sides together. Starting in one outside corner weave the outside edge.

See Square Frame Outside Edge graph for colors.

Bracelet with Square Frame

SIZE: 9" long

MATERIALS:

    84 Olivine 3mm bicone crystals

    48 Fuchsia 2xAB 3mm bicone crystals

    28 Lime 3mm bicone crystals

    4 Lime 4mm bicone crystals

    4 Fuchsia 4mm bicone crystals

    8mm Fuchsia AB cube crystal

    Smoke Fireline 4 lb. test

    5 Green Jade 15mm faceted rondelles

    12 Sterling Silver 6mm triangle spacer beads

    12 Sterling Silver 4mm round beads

    Sterling Silver toggle clasp

    4 Sterling Silver crimp tubes

    2 Sterling Silver crimp covers

    Softflex .014 diameter beading wire

INSTRUCTIONS:

    Make 1 complete Square Frame. Referring to photo, string bracelet components. Attach clasps and secure with crimp beads.

Square Frame

Attractive frames enhance the quality and announce the value of our favorite treasures. String a special square crystal into the center for special shimmer.

Tip: This beautiful frame can be used as a diamond or as a square depending on the location of the holes for stringing. On the bracelet, the corner edge beads were omitted (both inside and outside) on opposite corners to string it in a diamond shape.

SIZE: 1" x 1"

MATERIALS FOR 3MM SQUARE FRAME:

    84 Mint Alabaster 3mm bicone crystals

    52 Ruby 3mm bicone crystals

    24 Palace Green Opal 3mm bicone crystals

    Smoke Fireline 4 lb. test

    Beading needles (size 12 Sharps, size 15)

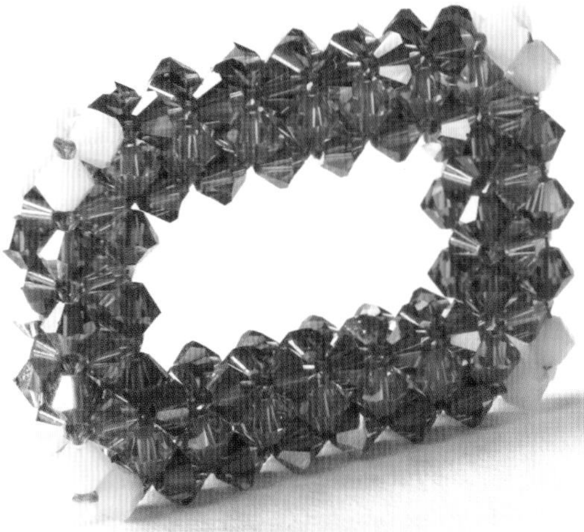

Rectangle Frame

Celebrate the beauty of a shape the ancient Greeks named "Golden".

Rectangle frames are lovely in any color and the accent corners add a hint of the natural shading found in flowers.

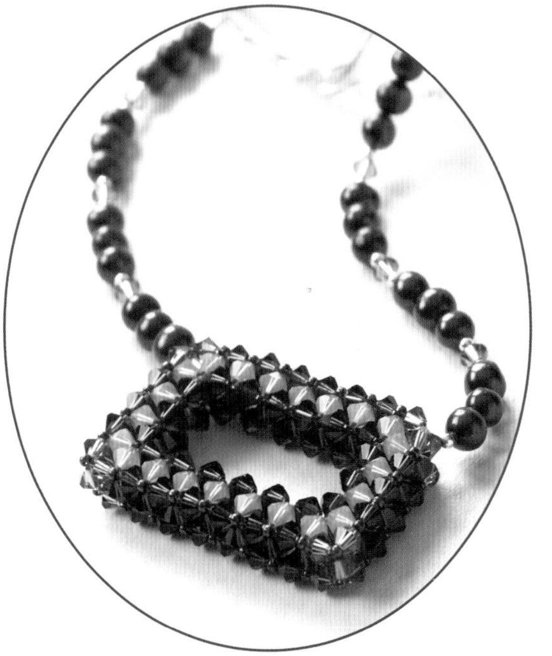

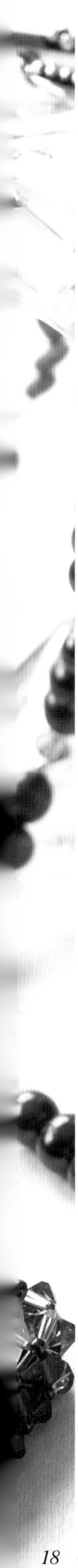

Rectangle Frame Outside Edge Graph

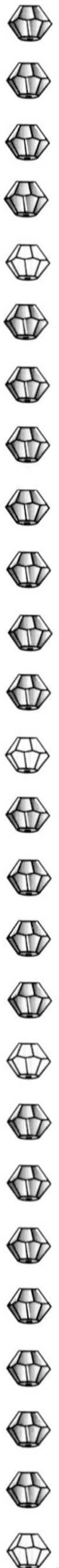

Start with this end.

SIZE: 1 1/4" x 1 3/4"

MATERIALS FOR 4MM RECTANGLE FRAME:

- 112 Fuchsia AB 4mm bicone crystals
- 44 Rose 4mm bicone crystals
- 20 Rose Alabaster 4mm bicone crystals
- Smoke Fireline 4 lb. test
- Beading needles (size 12 Sharps, size 15)

INSTRUCTIONS:

Weaving: Using the basic Right Angle Weave Frame instructions on page 6 and the Rectangle Frame Side graph, weave 2 rectangle sides.

Attaching the Edge: Refer to Attaching the Edge instructions on page 7. Use Fuchsia AB crystals for the inside edge.

Stack one side on top of the other. With the thread exiting one crystal on one of the sides, start in one corner on the inside of the rectangle to join the two sides together.

Starting in one outside corner weave the outside edge.

Refer to the Rectangle Frame Outside Edge graph for colors.

Fuchsia AB

Rose

Rose Alabaster

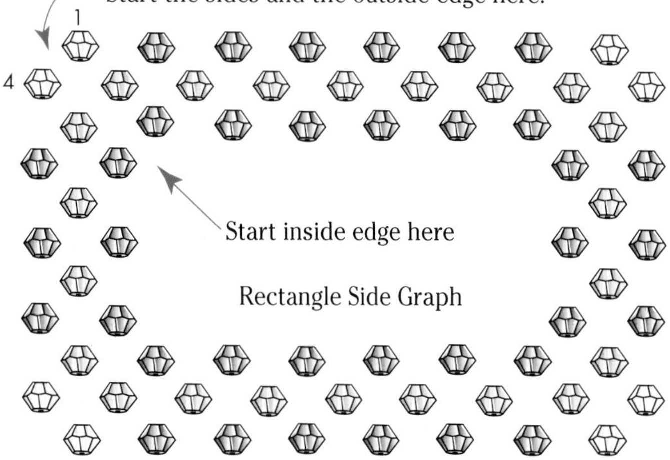

Rectangle Side Graph

Necklace with Rectangle Frame

SIZE: 18" long

MATERIALS:

- 112 Purple Velvet 4mm bicone crystals
- 44 Violet Opal 4mm bicone crystals
- 36 Tanzanite 4mm bicone crystals
- 48 Dark Purple 8mm round freshwater pearls
- 34 Sterling Silver 3mm round beads
- Sterling Silver toggle clasp
- 4 Sterling Silver crimp tubes
- Softflex .014 diameter beading wire
- Smoke Fireline 4 lb. test

INSTRUCTIONS:

Make 1 complete Rectangle Frame.

Necklace:

Referring to the photo, string necklace components.

Attach toggle clasps and secure with crimp tubes.

3mm bicone crystals   4mm bicone crystals

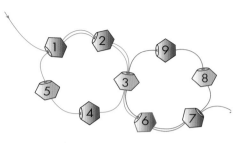

2. String crystals 6, 7, 8 and 9.
   Go through crystals 3, 6 and 7.

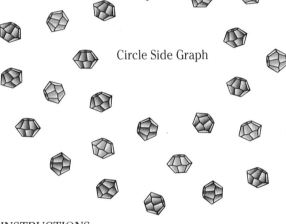

Circle Side Graph

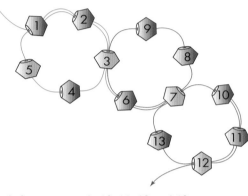

3. String crystals 10, 11, 12 and 13.
   Go through crystals 7, 10, 11 and 12.

INSTRUCTIONS:

Weaving:

   Using the Right Angle Weave Circle instructions and circle side graph, weave 2 circle sides.

            Dark Red Coral   ▮

            Lt. Topaz AB   ▯

Right Angle Weave (RAW) Circle Instructions

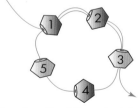

1. On a length of thread, string crystals 1, 2, 3, 4 and 5.

   Go through crystals 1, 2 and 3. This makes one unit.

4. Keep adding crystals four at a time until you have eight units (crystals 14 – 33).

   With the thread exiting crystal 31, string crystals 34 and 35 and go through crystal 5. String crystal 36 and go through crystal 31.

   This closes the circle.

Attaching the Edge:

   Refer to Attaching the Edge instructions on page 7.

   Stack one side on top of the other. With the thread exiting one crystal on one of the sides, start at any point on the inside of the circle to join the two sides together.

   Start at any point on the outside of the circle to weave the outside edge. Use Lt. Topaz AB crystals on both edges.

Necklace with Circle Pendant

SIZE: 19" long

MATERIALS:

58 Turquoise 4mm bicone crystals

2 Turquoise 3mm bicone crystals

29 Blue Zircon 4mm bicone crystals

6mm Crystal AB diamond shaped pendant

70 White Rice Potato 6mm freshwater pearls

8 Sterling Silver 3mm round beads

Sterling Silver toggle clasp

4 Sterling Silver crimp beads

Softflex .014 diameter beading wire

Smoke Fireline 4 lb. test

INSTRUCTIONS:

Make 1 complete Circle component.

Necklace:

Referring to the photo, string necklace components on beading wire.

Attach toggle clasps and secure with crimp beads.

Circle

Captivating shimmer keeps your eye moving across the fascinating facets of this bewitching pendant.

As the symbol of infinity, the circle enjoys a favored place in the hearts and minds of designers. Since ancient times jewelry makers have employed the circle in their art, introducing new styles and color combinations that are ever fresh.

Whether your style is contemporary or traditional, formal or informal, a circle pendant is always a fitting style.

SIZE: 1 1/8" x 1 1/8"

MATERIALS FOR 4MM CORAL CIRCLE:

Note: This project can also be made with 3mm bicone crystals. The 3mm sample uses 18 Matte Opaque Olive Gold 15/0 seed beads.

54 Dark Red Coral 4mm bicone crystals (or Palace Green Opal 3mm)

27 Lt. Topaz AB 4mm bicone crystals (or Amethyst 3mm)

Smoke Fireline 4 lb. test

Beading needles (size 12 Sharps, size 15)

Toggle Clasp

The Toggle Clasp is a combination of two parts, a Square Frame and a Bar.

It looks beautiful used as the focal feature of a bracelet or necklace. Simply make both pieces, then string them together with assorted beads for a fabulous piece of jewelry.

Bracelet with Toggle Clasp

SIZE: 9"

MATERIALS:

Red and Gold Toggle Clasp:

118 Dark Red Coral 3mm bicone crystals

87 Topaz 3mm bicone crystals

25 Light Colorado Topaz 3mm bicone crystals

6 Dark Red Coral 4mm bicone crystals

1 gram size 15/0 Matte Opaque Dark Red seed beads

5 Lemon Quartz 23mm freeform faceted beads

11 Gold-filled 4.5mm spacer beads

2 Gold-filled crimp tubes

2 Gold-filled crimp covers

Softflex .014 dia. beading wire

Smoke Fireline 4 lb. test

Beading needles
(size 12 Sharps, size 15)

INSTRUCTIONS:

Make 1 complete Toggle Clasp.

Bracelet:

Referring to the photo, string bracelet components onto beading wire.

Attach toggle clasps and secure with crimp tubes.

Start here

↓

SIZE: 1" x 1"

MATERIALS FOR 3MM TOGGLE CLASP:

118 Montana 3mm bicone crystals

85 Ruby 3mm bicone crystals

25 Crystal Copper 3mm bicone crystals

1 gram size 15/0 matte Gunmetal seed beads

Smoke Fireline 4 lb. test

Beading needles (size 12 Sharps, size 15)

Toggle
Clasp
Square
Frame
Outside
Edge
Graph

Start sides and outside edge here

1

4

Start inside edge here

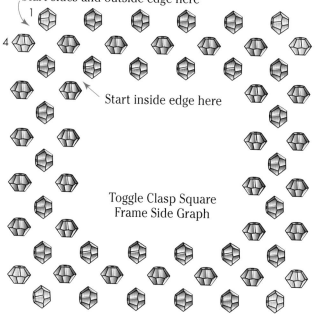

Toggle Clasp Square
Frame Side Graph

INSTRUCTIONS:

Square Frame for Toggle Clasp Weaving:

Using the basic Frame instructions on page 6 and the Toggle Clasp Square Frame Side graph, weave 2 square frame sides.

Attaching the Edge:

Refer to the Attaching the Edge instructions on page 7.

Use Ruby crystals on the inside edge. Stack one side on top of the other. With the thread exiting one crystal on one of the sides, start in one corner on the inside of the square to join the two sides together.

Starting in one outside corner weave the outside edge. See Toggle Clasp Square Frame Outside Edge graph for colors.

Attach the Loop:

1. With the thread exiting one corner crystal of the outside edge, string seven 15/0 seed beads and take the needle through the other side of the crystal.

Note: You may stop here and eliminate steps 2 and 3 if you want.

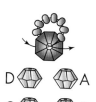

D   A

C   B

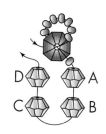

D   A

C   B

2. Go back through the seven 15/0 seed beads. String one 15/0 seed bead and take the needle through side crystals A, B, C and D.

3. String one 15/0 seed bead and take the needle through the loop of seven 15/0 seed beads. This will bring the thread out on the other side of the square frame. Add the two 15/0 seed beads for this side in the same way.

Start here in one corner of toggle bar

↓

Toggle Bar Top Side Graph

Toggle Bar Bottom Side Graph

Bar for Toggle Clasp:

Using the basic Right Angle Weave instructions on page 5 and Toggle Bar Top Side and Bottom Side graphs, weave one toggle bar top and one toggle bar bottom. Each is eight units long.

Refer to the Attaching the Edge instructions on page 7. Stack 1 side on top of the other. With the thread exiting one crystal on one of the sides, start at one end to join the two sides together. Attach the other edge.

Refer to Edge Graph for colors.

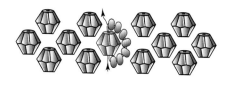

Attaching Loop:

With the thread exiting the center crystal on the bottom of the bar, string seven 15/0 seed beads.

Go through the other side of the center crystal.

Crystal Copper ▢

Montana ▢

Ruby ▢

Toggle Bar
Edge Graph

Crystals with Right Angle Weave 23

Necklace with Cross

SIZE: 18" long

MATERIALS:

Red-Orange Cross:

    56 Indian Red 4mm bicone crystals

    38 Fire Opal 4mm bicone crystals

    8 Topaz 4mm bicone crystals

    2 grams size 11/0 Orange/Yellow seed beads

    48 Gold 8mm potato shaped freshwater pearls

    Gold-filled Push-Pull clasp

    2 Gold-filled crimp tubes

    Softflex .014 dia. beading wire

    Smoke Fireline 4 lb. test

    Beading needles
        (size 12 Sharps, size 15)

INSTRUCTIONS:

    Make 1 Cross pendant.

Necklace:

    Referring to the photo, string the necklace components.

    Attach Push-Pull clasp and secure with crimp tubes.

3mm bicone crystals   4mm bicone crystals

Cross
for Pendants and Earrings

As an traditional cultural motif, the cross has been around longer than the pyramids and the continued popularity of this design is undeniable. Nearly every culture on the planet has attached some significance to this design and the lore is both interesting and extensive. As an artform, this design offers endless possibilities for combining color and texture and these elements influence the style of the finished work. Although the size of the pendant will vary with the size of the chosen crystals, the elegance of every design remains constant.

Cross Side Graph

Start here →

Lime ☐
Black Diamond 2xAB ◨
Purple Velvet ■

Start edge here →

SIZE: 1¼" x 1¾"

MATERIALS FOR 4MM CROSS:

Note: This project can also be made with 3mm bicone crystals.

    56 Black Diamond 2xAB 4mm bicone crystals (or Olivine 3mm)

    38 Purple Velvet 4mm bicone crystals (or Pacific Opal 3mm)

    8 Lime 4mm bicone crystals (or Metallic Blue 3mm)

    1 gram size 15/0 Opaque Eggplant Luster seed beads
        (or Matte Opaque Dark Blue seed beads for 3mm sample)

    Smoke Fireline 4 lb. test

    Beading needles (size 12 Sharps, size 15)

Cross continued

INSTRUCTIONS:

Weaving:

Using the Cross instructions and Cross graph, weave two cross sides.

Attaching the Edge:

Refer to the Attaching the Edge instructions on page 7.

Use Black Diamond 2xAB crystals for the edge, except on the four points where you will substitute three 15/0 seed beads for the two crystals on each point. Stack one side on top of the other.

With the thread exiting one crystal on one side, start at the bottom point of the cross to join the two sides together.

Tip: When using 3mm crystals, use two 15/0 seed beads instead of three on the edge of the points.

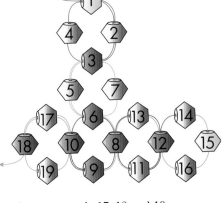

Right Angle Weave (RAW) Cross Instructions

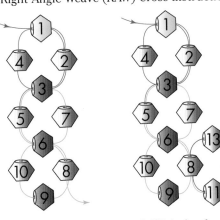

Refer to the basic Right Angle Weave instructions on page 5.

1. Weave a single row - 3 units long.

2. With the thread exiting crystal 8, string crystals 11, 12 and 13.
   Go through crystals 8, 11 and 12.

3. String crystals 14, 15 and 16.
   Go through crystals 12, 13, 8, 9 and 10.

4. String crystals 17, 18 and 19.
   Go through crystals 10, 17 and 18.

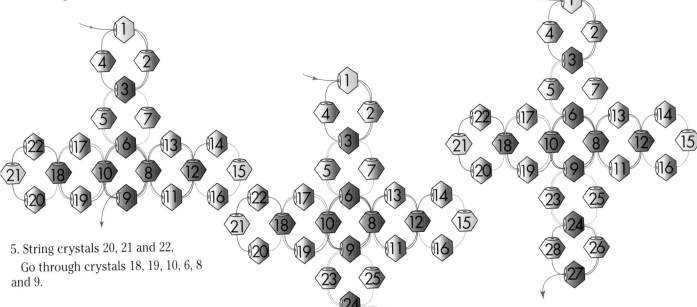

5. String crystals 20, 21 and 22.
   Go through crystals 18, 19, 10, 6, 8 and 9.

6. String crystals 23, 24 and 25.
   Go through crystals 9, 23 and 24.

7. String crystals 26, 27 and 28.
   Go through crystals 24, 26 and 27.

8. String crystals 29, 30 and 31.
   Go through crystals 27, 29 and 30.

9. String crystals 32, 33 and 34.
   Go through crystal 30.

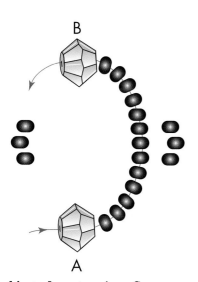

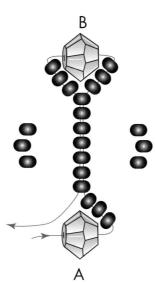

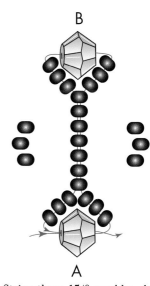

Attaching a Loop to a 4mm Cross:

1. With the thread exiting one of the side crystals (A) of the top point of the cross, string thirteen 15/0 seed beads.

   Take the needle through the opposite side crystal (B).

2. String three 15/0 seed beads. Skipping the last three 15/0 seed beads strung in the previous thirteen.

   Take the needle through the next seven 15/0 seed beads.

3. String three 15/0 seed beads.

   Take the needle through crystal A.

Attach a Loop to a 3mm Cross:

Note: When making a 3mm project, you need to change the 15/0 seed bead counts to:
   Step 1 - nine 15/0 seed beads
   Step 2 - String two 15/0 seed beads. Take the needle through five 15/0 seed beads. String two 15/0 seed beads.

3mm bicone crystals   4mm bicone crystals

Triangle Bail

Why purchase plain silver when you can have tantalizing sparkle? Create a finding that complements your necklace and enhances the opulence of its pendant with this glamorous Triangle Bail.

One of the most stable structures of all, the triangle here transcends the boundaries of artistic design and assumes its rightful place amongst your favorite bejeweled accessories.

Perfect for attaching a stunning crystal to a necklace, this bail is both fabulous and functional.

4mm SIZE: $^7/_8$" x 1$^1/_8$"
3mm SIZE: $^5/_8$" x $^7/_8$"

MATERIALS FOR 4MM BAIL:

Tip: This project can also be made with 3mm bicone crystals.
    20 Erinite 4mm bicone crystals (or Padparadshca 3mm)
    16 Violet Opal 4mm bicone crystals (or Mint Alabaster 3mm)
    1 gram size 15/0 Matte Opaque Lilac seed beads
        (or Matte Opaque Sea Foam Luster seed beads for 3mm sample)
    Crystal Fireline 4 lb. test
    Beading needles (size 12 Sharps, size 15)

INSTRUCTIONS:
Weaving:

    Using the Right Angle Weave Triangle Bail instructions on pages 30-31 and the Triangle Bail graph, weave one triangle bail.

Erinite ⬜
Violet Opal ⬜

Necklace with Triangle Bail

SIZE: 18" long

MATERIALS:
    20 Pink Alabaster 3mm
        bicone crystals
    20 Emerald 2xAB 3mm
        bicone crystals
    12 Emerald 2xAB 4mm
        bicone crystals
    Crystal AB 16mm Baroque
        crystal pendant
    1 gram size 13/0 Opaque Blue/Green
        AB Charlotte seed beads
    18 Rose Quartz 12mm barrel beads
    36 Sterling Silver 5mm square
        spacer beads
    32 Sterling Silver 4mm round beads
    8 Sterling Silver 2mm round beads
    Sterling Silver toggle clasp
    4 Sterling Silver crimp tubes
    2 Sterling Silver crimp covers
    Soft Touch .010 dia beading wire
    Crystal Fireline 4 lb. test
    Beading needles
        (size 12 Sharps, size 15)

INSTRUCTIONS:
    Make 1 Triangle Bail.
Necklace:
    Referring to the photo, string necklace components onto beading wire.
    Attach toggle clasp and secure with crimp beads and covers.

Start beading here

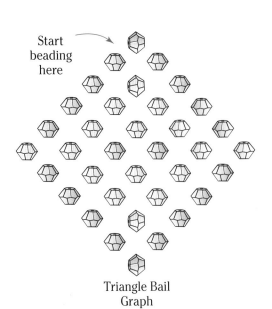

Triangle Bail
Graph

Triangle Bail continued

INSTRUCTIONS:

Weaving:

Using the Right Angle Weave Triangle Bail instructions and the Triangle Bail Graph, weave beads following diagrams 1 through 9 to form a bail.

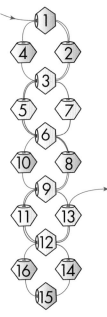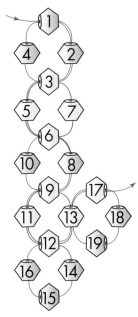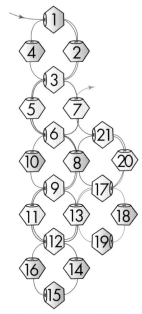

1. Refer to the basic Right Angle Weave instructions on page 5. Weave a single row of beadwork 5 units long.

2. With the thread exiting crystal 13, string crystals 17, 18 and 19.

   Go through 13 and 17.

3. String crystals 20 and 21.

   Go through crystals 8, 17, 20, 21 and 7.

4. String crystals 22 and 23.

   Go through crystals 21, 8, 17 and 20.

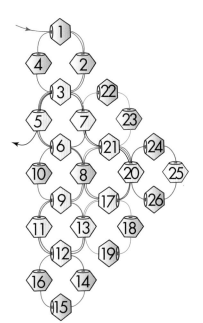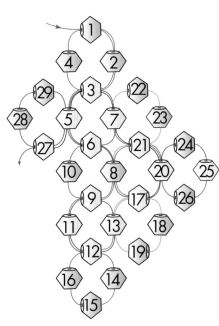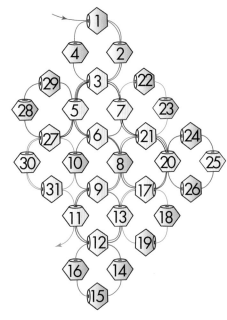

5. String crystals 24, 25 and 26.

   Go through crystals 20, 21 7, 3 and 5.

6. String crystals 27, 28 and 29.

   Go through crystals 5 and 27.

7. String crystals 30 and 31.

   Go through crystals 10, 27, 30, 31 and 11.

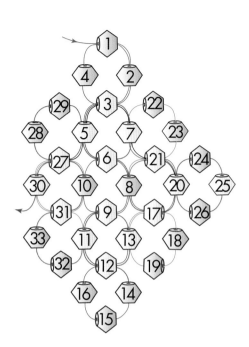

8. String crystals 32 and 33.
   Go through crystals 31, 10, 27 and 30.

9. String crystals 34, 35 and 36.
   Go through crystal 30.

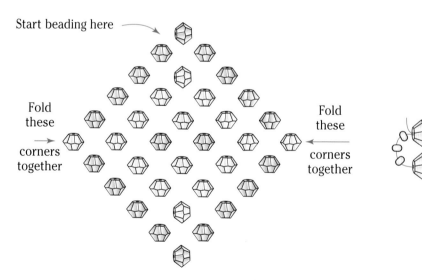

Start beading here

Fold these → corners together

Fold these ← corners together

Triangle Bail:

Refer to the Right Angle Weave instructions and Triangle Bail graph.

Fold the beadwork in half so that the two Violet Opal crystal corners (top and bottom) touch and make a point.

Connect these two Violet Opal crystals by adding 15/0 seed beads between them. With the thread exiting crystal A, string three 15/0 seed beads and go through crystal B. String three 15/0 seed beads and go through crystal A. (Diagram)

Tip: If you are working with 3mm crystals, use two 15/0 seed beads instead of three on each side.

Attach the Loop:

Refer to the Attaching Loop instructions for the Cross Component on page 27.

Make a loop at the bottom point (two Violet Opal crystals) of the Triangle Bail.

Gallery

These advanced jewelry designs were created using techniques and components found in this book.

Dangling Earrings

No accessory wardrobe is complete without a pair of gleaming chandelier earrings. A gorgeous solid square supports delicate drops of crystalline sparkle weightlessly suspended from silver link chain.

Bracelet with Squares

Square frames and a toggles feature a glorious combination of amethyst and topaz crystals that will definitely light up the night.

This twinkling bracelet is a radiant example of how the components in this book can be merged to produce spectacular results.

Necklace with Toggle Clasp

Classic and classy, this glittering necklace moves readily from every day office wear to an enchanted evening out on the town. The gorgeous crystal toggle clasp made with the square technique provides the perfect finale on a necklace that is destined to be noticed and appreciated.

Gallery

These advanced jewelry designs were created using techniques and components found in this book.

Cross Earrings

Turn a twinkling cross into an exquisite pair of earrings.

This pair is a perfect stand-alone accessory or you can easily add a matching pendant or pin for a spirited trio.

Bracelet
with Toggle Clasp

Shimmer and shine place this chic bracelet in a class by itself.

A step above the ordinary, this appealing piece is flashy and glamorous and must be worn by those who are not afraid to be noticed.